# MEL BAY'S COMPLETE DOUBLE BASS DRUM COOKBOOK

### By Rocky Neill

GW00672177

A cassette tape and compact disc of the music in this book are now available. The publisher strongly recommends the use of one of these recordings along with the text to insure accuracy of interpretation and ease in learning.

BD 1 = RIGHT FOOT BASS DRUM

BD 2 = LEFT FOOT

# PART I

Double bass is the most exciting new horizon for drummers today. I call it new because only recently has anyone started testing its limits and understanding its potential. When double bass is played in the right spot in a song or during a solo, it pushes the excitement level of the audience to new heights. I have recently been accused of having my bass drum part on audio tape by an audience member because they didn't understand how one bass drum could produce that much sound. (I play a single bass with a double pedal). I consider it a backhanded type of compliment (but I'll take it!). Creating the illusion is what excites the audience, because they instinctively try to figure out how you did it, like trying to figure out how a magician's trick works.

*Complete Double Bass Cookbook* is a book designed to get the beginner going in the right direction but at the same time to challenge the intermediate to advanced players. The level of difficulty is determined by the metronome setting used while practicing the exercises. Obviously the beginner will want to practice at slower tempos while the more advanced players will want to go for speed. If you don't have a metronome, go out and get one. Developing good time is critical to good playing. The metronome "click" will also fill the gap created when the rest is on "one" of the measure.

The best way to use this book is to practice one page per day, marking the date of completion and metronome speed. Try to be as consistent as possible about practicing.

To develop control and the ability to start and stop these patterns, each of the fifteen cymbal patterns is combined with five different foot patterns; those being no rest, then resting on the fourth, the third, the second, and finally on the first beat of the measure. After you have played all five patterns, the cymbal pattern changes and you will start the five-step process all over again. As the book progresses, the final exercises will be much easier to play if you use a metronome and set the "click" to a quarter note setting. This way, the "click" will fill the void created when neither the cymbal, snare drum, or bass drums are played exactly on the pulse of each measure.

# PRACTICE TIPS

After you have completed an entire page, go back and do each exercise four times and then go on to the next one without stopping, until you have completed the whole page.

Also, after completing the entire book, start over and kick up the metronome speed 15-20 beats per minute faster than the first time. By now, the first hand patterns will seem much easier and enable you to play the figures faster. This is where the rubber meets the road; where you should start to get ideas for practical applications for these patterns in whatever style of music you play. This book is really meant to help you develop your technique or "chops" but occasionally you will play a given pattern and think "Hey, that would be a nice groove to use in that song my band is working on."

Just for fun, after you feel comfortable with the four sixteenth-note pattern, try to increase your speed by using both hands on the closed hi-hat. Obviously you won't be able to play the hi-hat and snare at the same time, but the the over and under action of the hands might give you some interesting ideas.

Also, to further develop your dexterity and get more mileage out of this book, experiment with reversing the hands and/or the feet. It will seem wierd at first, but I have found that "role reversal" on the drumset conditions you to play difficult patterns with much greater ease when you go back to the original hand/foot configuration. Try it!

Be sure to read the sections about leg conditioning and bass drum tuning. The subjects brought up in these sections could save you a lot of time by bringing up points you might not have considered before.

Another point I'd like to bring up is whether or not your secondary foot keeps the beater pressed against the head when not in use. This is a common problem for double bass players. Try it yourself and see if you do it. The reason this occurs when you switch from single to double bass is that your hi-hat (or secondary) foot is conditioned to keep the hi-hat closed whenever it's not in use. After doing this for years in most cases, it's a hard habit to break. When using a single bass drum with a double pedal, the dominant beater will be hindered if the secondary beater is always pressed against the head just an inch away. If you just can't break this habit, the best alternative is to play two bass drums with single pedals.

Here is the transcription key:

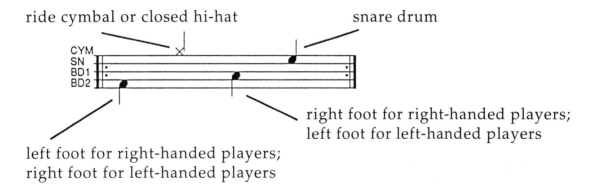

ride cymbal or closed hi-hat          snare drum

right foot for right-handed players;
left foot for left-handed players

left foot for right-handed players;
right foot for left-handed players

# LEG CONDITIONING

Here are some tips for toning the muscle groups in your legs that are used most when playing two bass drums (or one for that matter).

Daily exercise of these groups should help increase your speed, but more importantly your stamina. I prefer playing with my heels up, but generally I've observed half of the drummers with their heels up and half with heels down. There is an advantage for the heel-up players because they have the ability to utilize a third muscle group not used by the heel-down players. I'm not trying to convert the heel-down players, but just to present the facts on a subject critical to playing well but often neglected. You make the choice and see what works best for you.

Before trying any of the exercises suggested in this section, consult your physician.

LEG CONDITIONING FOR THE "HEEL-UP" PLAYER
Heel up: Utilizes a combination of three muscle groups:

A) Back of lower legs or calves (gastrocs and solens primarily) Figure 2
B) Front of upper leg or thigh; quadraceps (commonly called quads) Figure 3
C) Lower back muscles (iliopsoas muscles) Figure 3

I feel that the heel-up player has a distinct advantage because he or she can put the whole leg into the pedal instead of just utilizing the leg from the ankle down. This makes it possible to play with more volume without exerting much more energy. Another part of the anatomy that is crucial is the Achilles tendon. This is the thick tendon that attaches to the heel and runs up into the calf. It takes virtually no energy to keep this tendon contracted, thus lifting the heel off the pedal. When you do this, it enables you to "feather" your foot against the pedal and play faster figures and doubles that I have found much harder to play with my heels down.

To play double bass, you need to increase your stamina by developing the muscle groups listed above. You're not necessarily wanting to develop more strength, but more importantly the ability to play longer with less fatigue. (In other words, with increased stamina).

A good exercise for the heel-up player would be bicycle riding which utilizes each group of the muscles in a low-impact way. A light workout each day (even on an exer-cycle) will prepare you to play double bass with much greater ease. Just remember to be consistent with your workouts.

LEG CONDITIONING FOR THE "HEEL-DOWN" PLAYER
Heel down: Utilizes a combination of two muscle groups;

A) Front of lower leg (tibialis anterior primarily) Figure 1
B) Calves (gastrocs and solens) Figure 2

This type of player is somewhat at a disadvantage because of the use of only two of muscles and loss of a natural spring in the leg utilized by the heel-up player. The best exercise for the heel-down player is to practice or repeatedly exercise on the bass pedals themselves. This is because very few exercises imitate the motion better than itself. One good exercise to develop these muscle groups (if you have access to a weight-lifting machine) is to completely extend your legs on the leg press and with the top half of your feet actually touching the footboard, flex the ankles in and out very slowly. Start out with a moderate amount of weight. This is a great way for toning the ankles quickly and evenly.

# FIGURE ONE     FIGURE TWO     FIGURE THREE

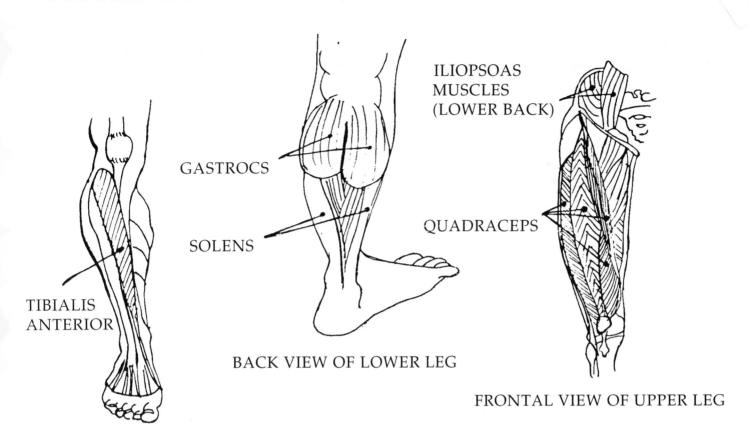

TIBIALIS
ANTERIOR

GASTROCS

SOLENS

ILIOPSOAS
MUSCLES
(LOWER BACK)

QUADRACEPS

BACK VIEW OF LOWER LEG

FRONTAL VIEW OF UPPER LEG

FRONT VIEW OF LOWER LEG

# BASS DRUM TUNING

Tuning is an area of drumming that everyone has their own definite opinions on and I am no exception. It seems like over the years, when I have taken advice about tuning my kit, it just never worked out the same even when I followed the directions exactly. All of the scientific theories and special gadgets in the world won't take the place of simply sitting down and adjusting and readjusting each tension rod while experimenting with different types of muffling in order to achieve the sound you desire. Since this book concentrates on the bass drums, I am going to focus on bass drum tuning. I have a method that works for me so give it a try if you're not happy with the sound of your bass drums. First off, you need to consider the laws of physics and how they play into this and how to use them to your advantage. My point being that the larger the head, the more flexibility it has and the less response (or bounce) you get. The good thing about the larger head is the deeper tone which is desirable for the bass drum. On the other side of the coin, the smaller head will give you more bounce enabling you to play faster figures with less effort, but you'll get higher pitch which is undesirable on the bass drum.

When I tune drums in general, I've always tuned them to achieve maximum response while at the same time coming as close as possible to the pitch that the drum was made for. There is no way to have both of these qualities in the extreme at the same time because, for example, if you crank the tension rods as tight as possible to achieve the fastest bounce, the drum will sound bad because the pitch will be much higher than the drum was made for. So my objective was to find that fine line where I get the maximum bounce while producing the best pitch possible, both at the same time. Now that I've bored you with a physics lesson, here's my combination of ingredients to attain the best sounding and most responsive bass drums possible.

The diameter I suggest is 20" with eight lugs on each side. The beater head I recommend is a Remo Clear Pinstripe. The front head should be a one-ply, (maybe a Clear Ambassador). Now, the next step would be to install a Remo "Muffl' Ring" inside the beater head after you have placed a 2" thick piece of foam, (about 18" long) along the bottom of the drum. It would also help to lay a small feather filled pillow on top of the piece of foam. The pillow and the foam piece should be laid long-ways along the bottom of the bass drum and not touch either head directly. The actual amount of tensioning on the tuning rods is up to you but I have gotten the best results when the front head is slightly tighter than the beater head.

Metronome Setting _____

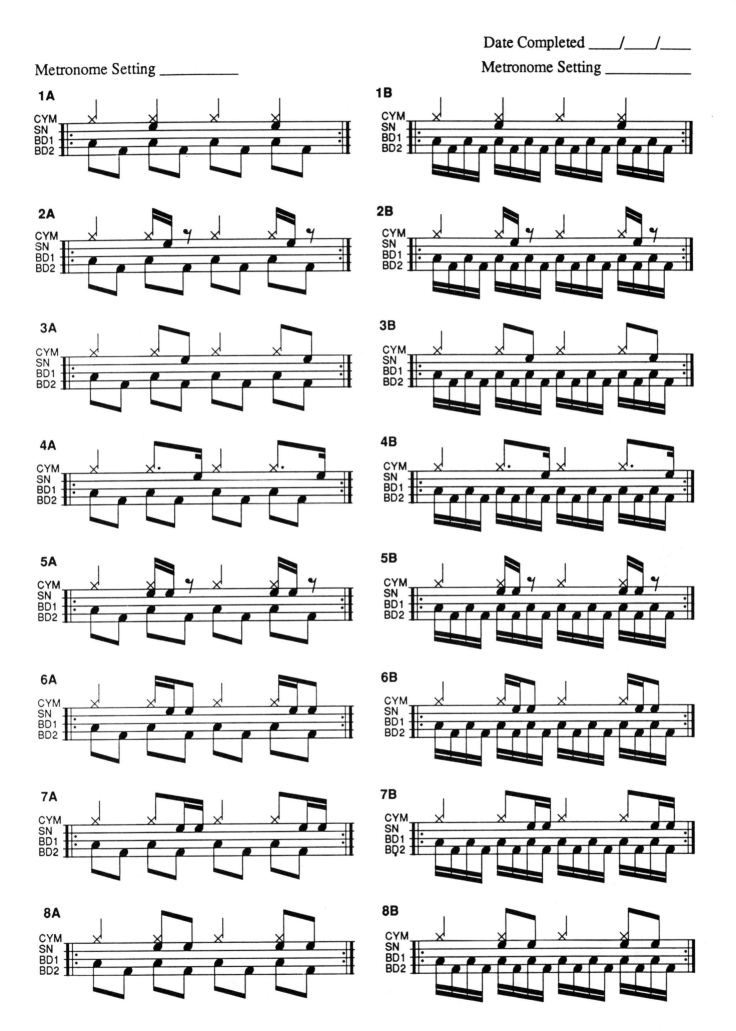

7

Metronome Setting _____

Metronome Setting _____

Metronome Setting _____

9

Metronome Setting _____

Metronome Setting _____

Metronome Setting _____

11

Metronome Setting _____

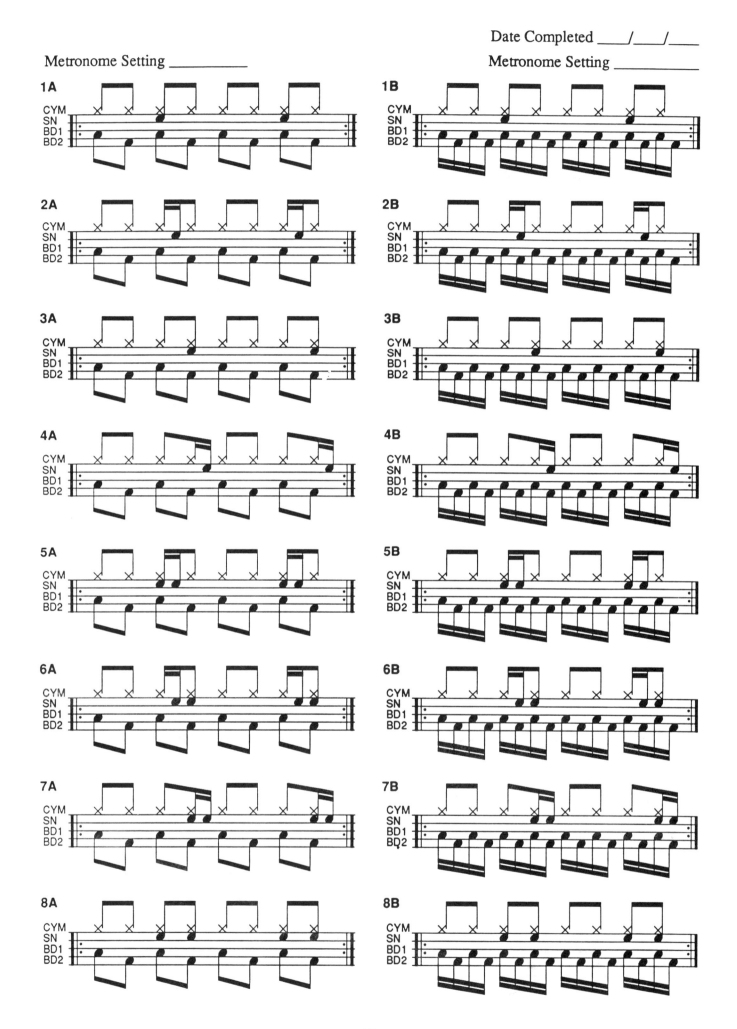

12

Metronome Setting _____

Metronome Setting _____

Metronome Setting _____

Metronome Setting _____

Metronome Setting _____

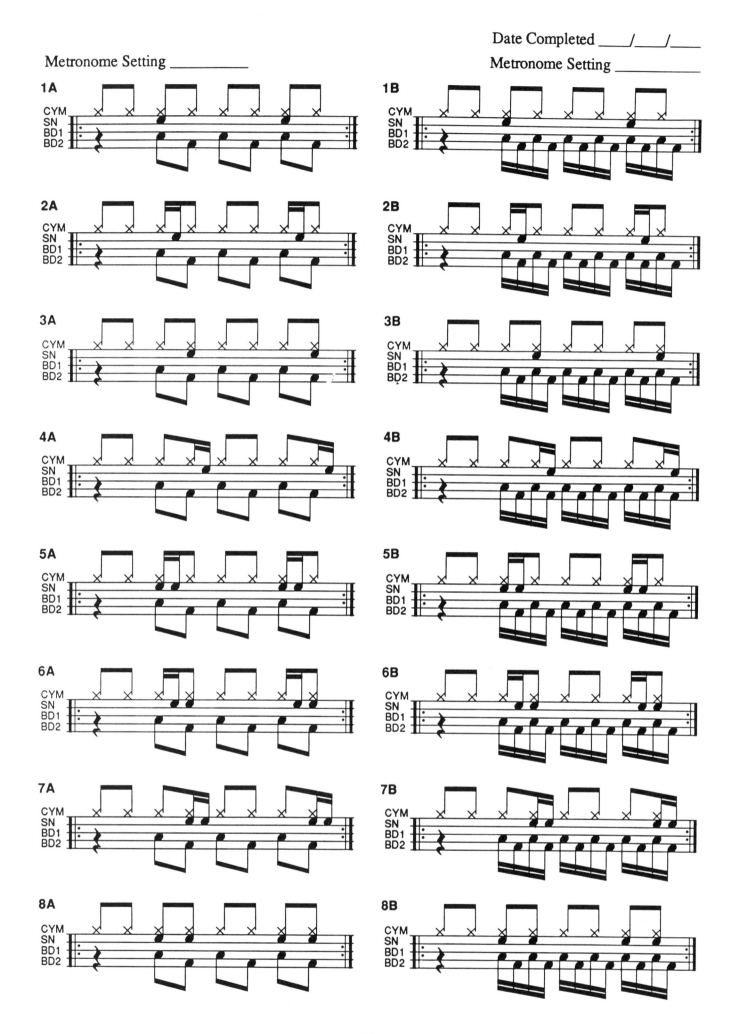

Metronome Setting _____

Metronome Setting _____

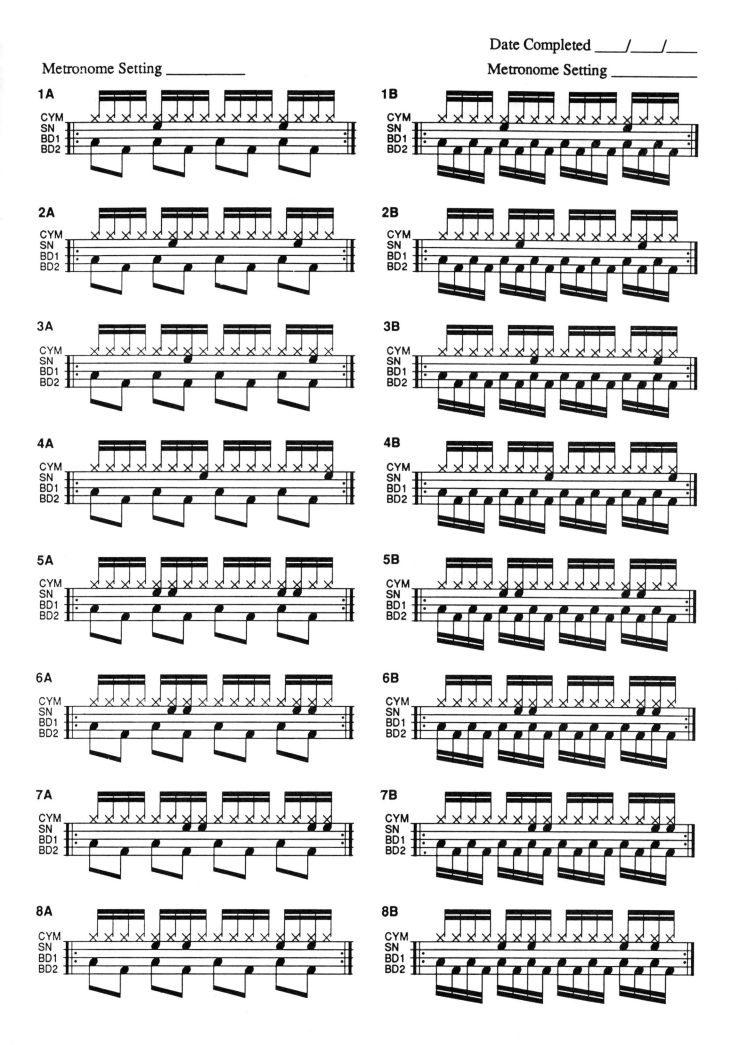

Metronome Setting _____

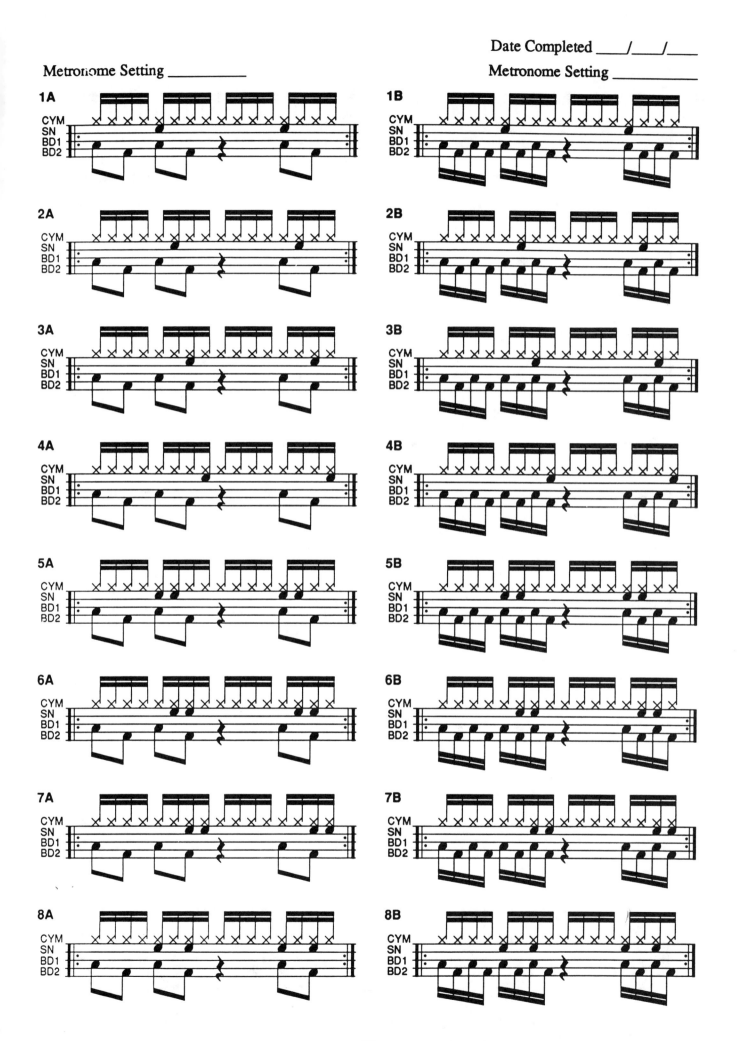

Metronome Setting _____     Metronome Setting _____

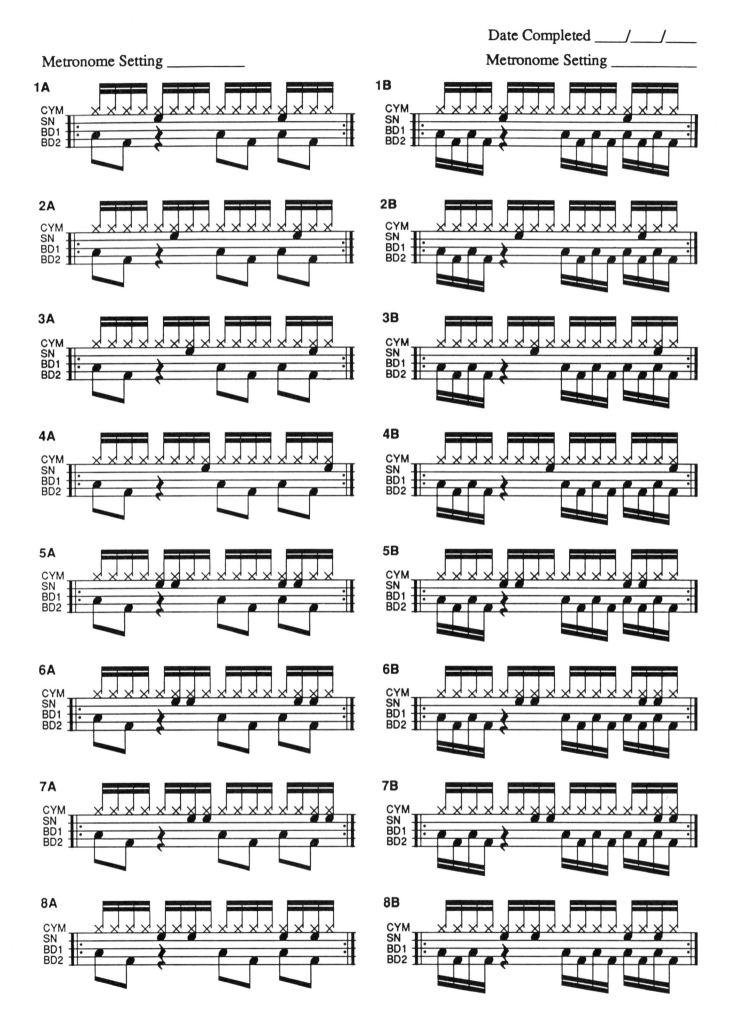

Metronome Setting _____

Metronome Setting _____

Metronome Setting _____

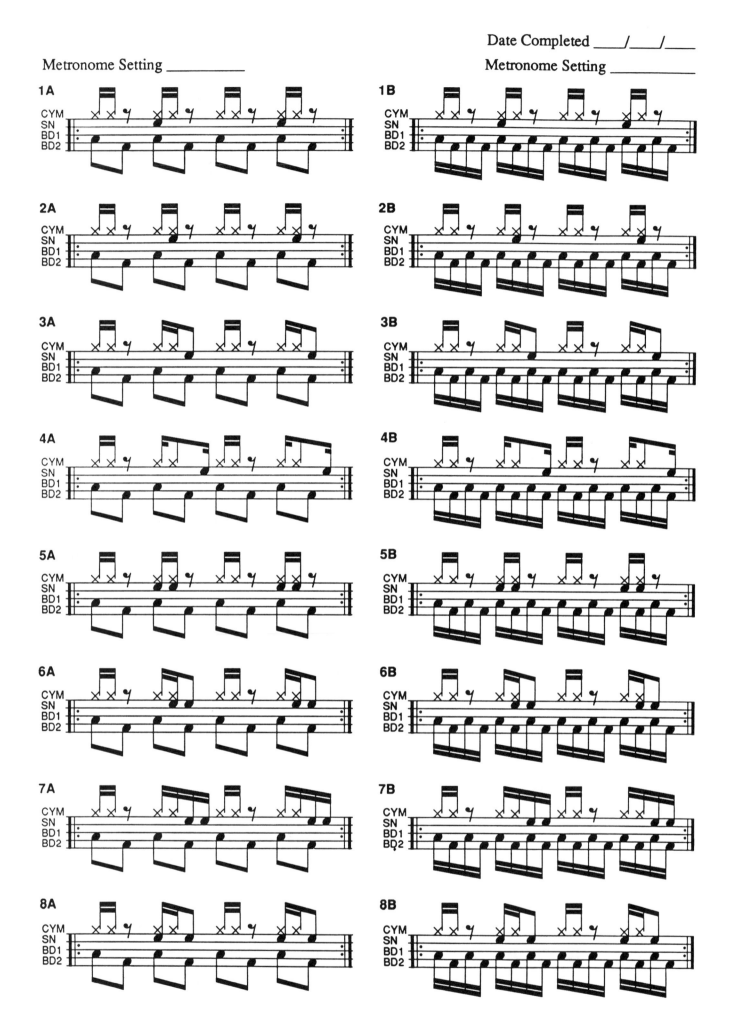

Metronome Setting _____

23

Metronome Setting _____                     Metronome Setting _____

24

Metronome Setting _____

Metronome Setting _____

Metronome Setting _____

26

Metronome Setting _____

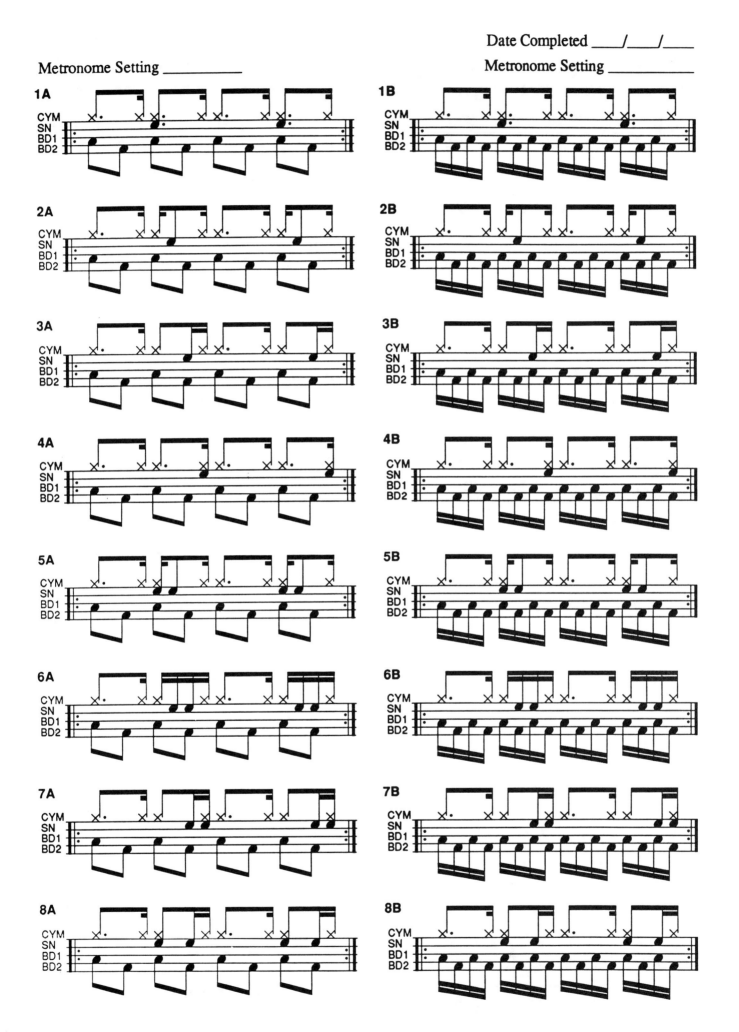

27

Metronome Setting _____

Metronome Setting _____

28

Metronome Setting _____                    Metronome Setting _____

29

Metronome Setting _____

Metronome Setting _____

Metronome Setting _____

Metronome Setting _____

Metronome Setting _____

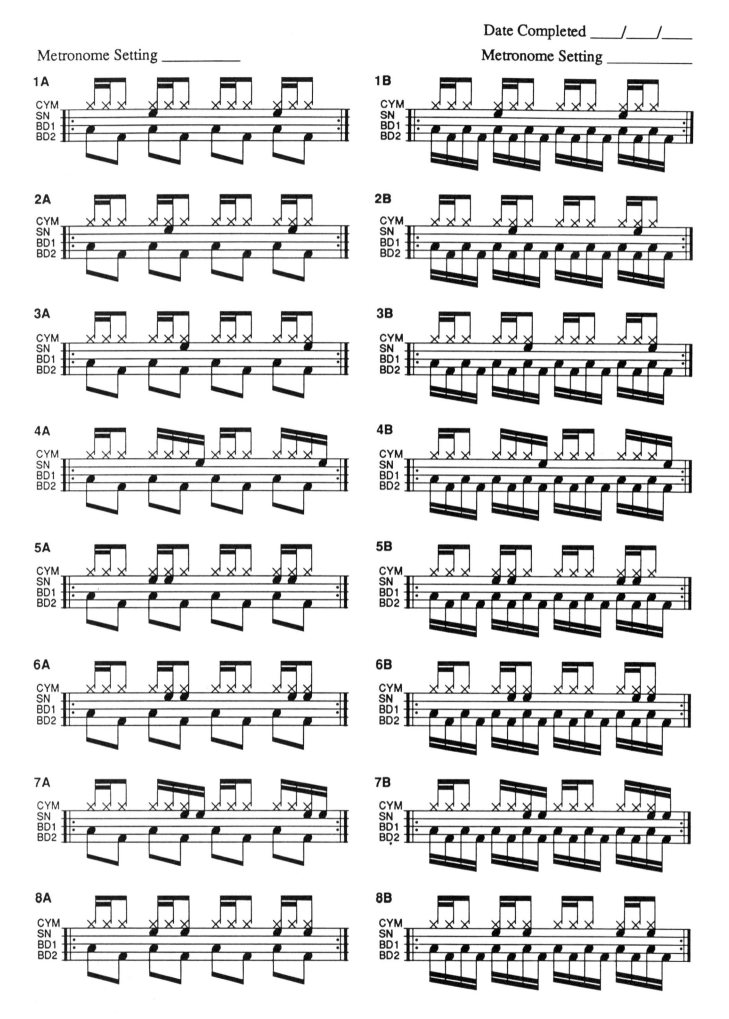

Metronome Setting _____

Date Completed ____/____/____

Metronome Setting _____

Metronome Setting _____

34

Metronome Setting _____          Metronome Setting _____

Metronome Setting _____

Metronome Setting _____

Metronome Setting _____          Metronome Setting _____

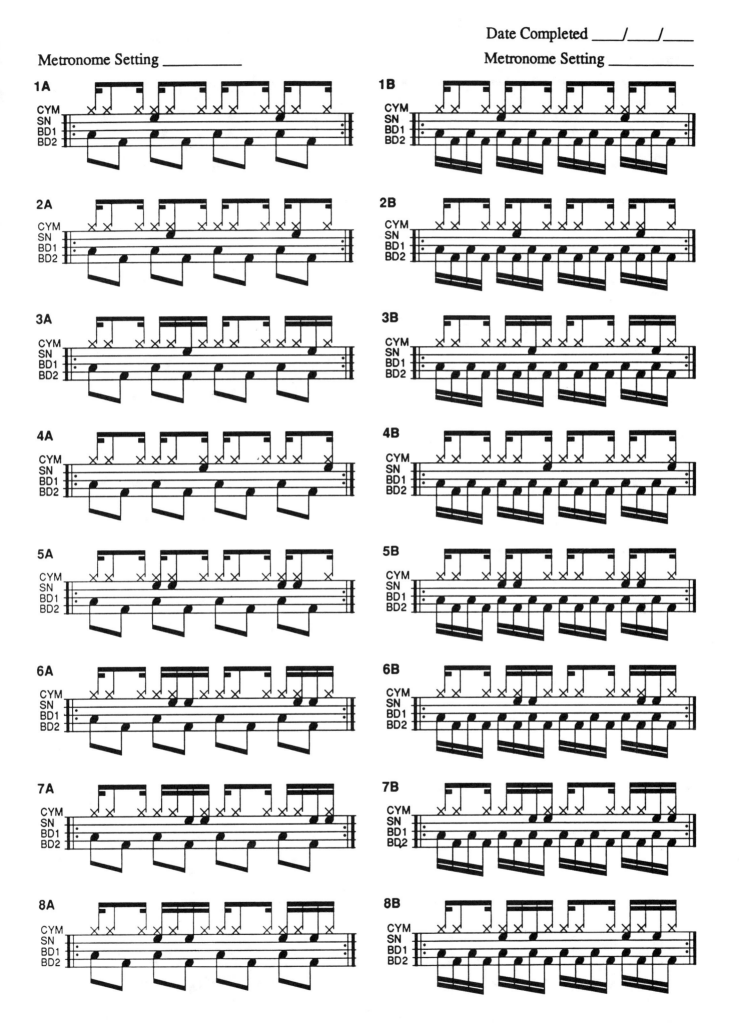

37

Metronome Setting _____

Metronome Setting _____

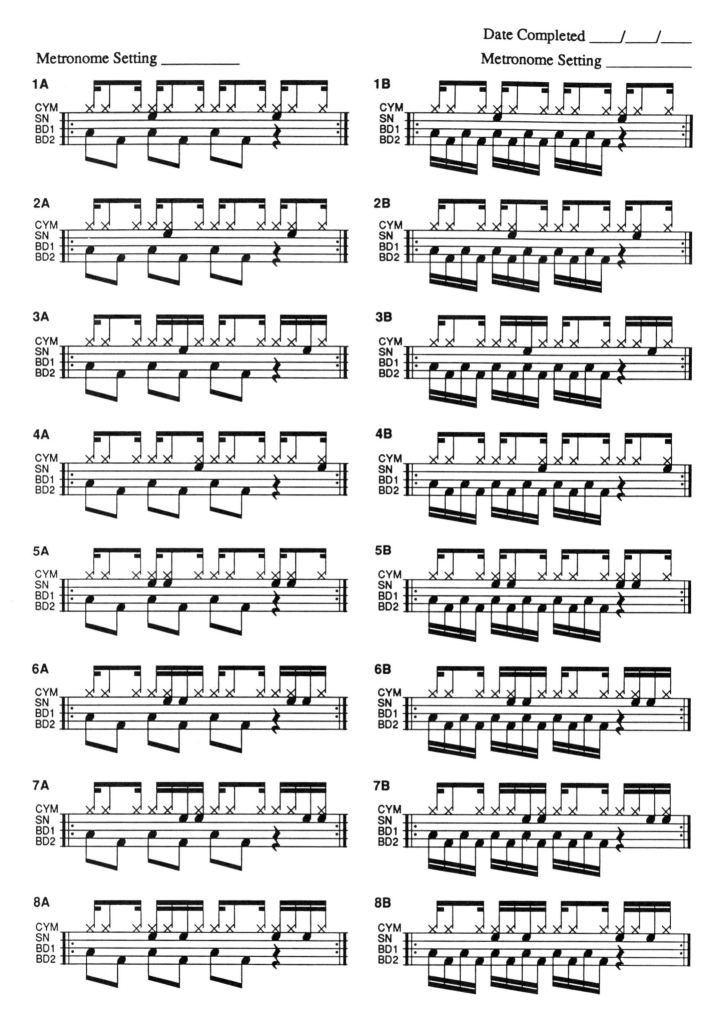

38

Metronome Setting _____

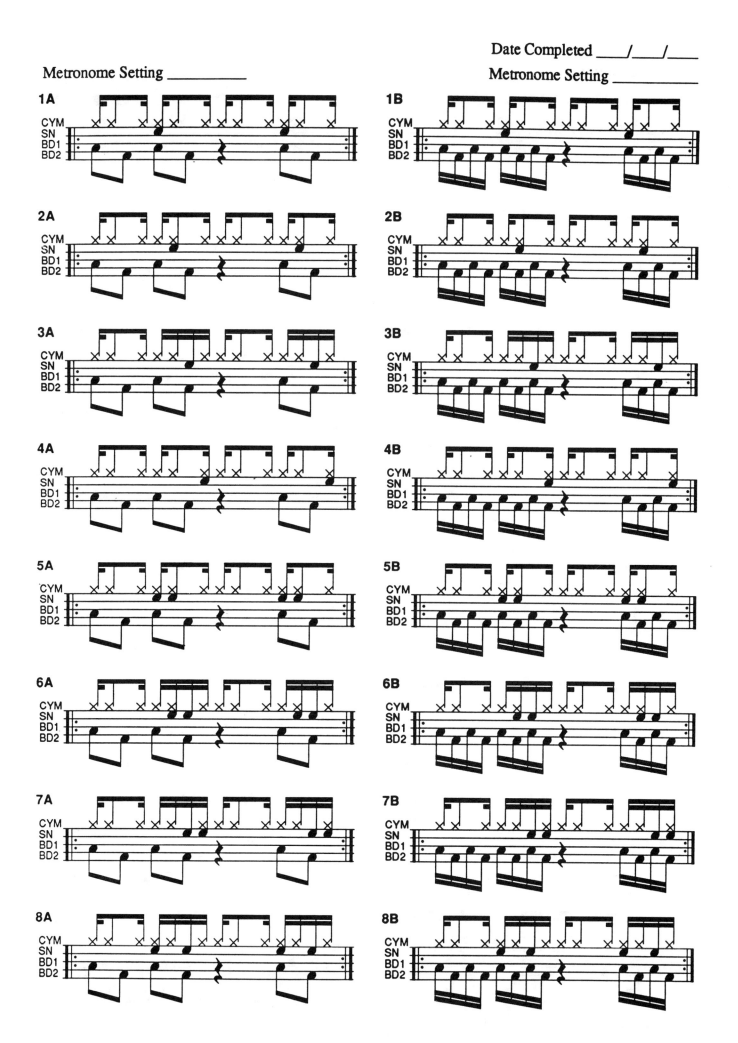

Metronome Setting _____

Metronome Setting _____

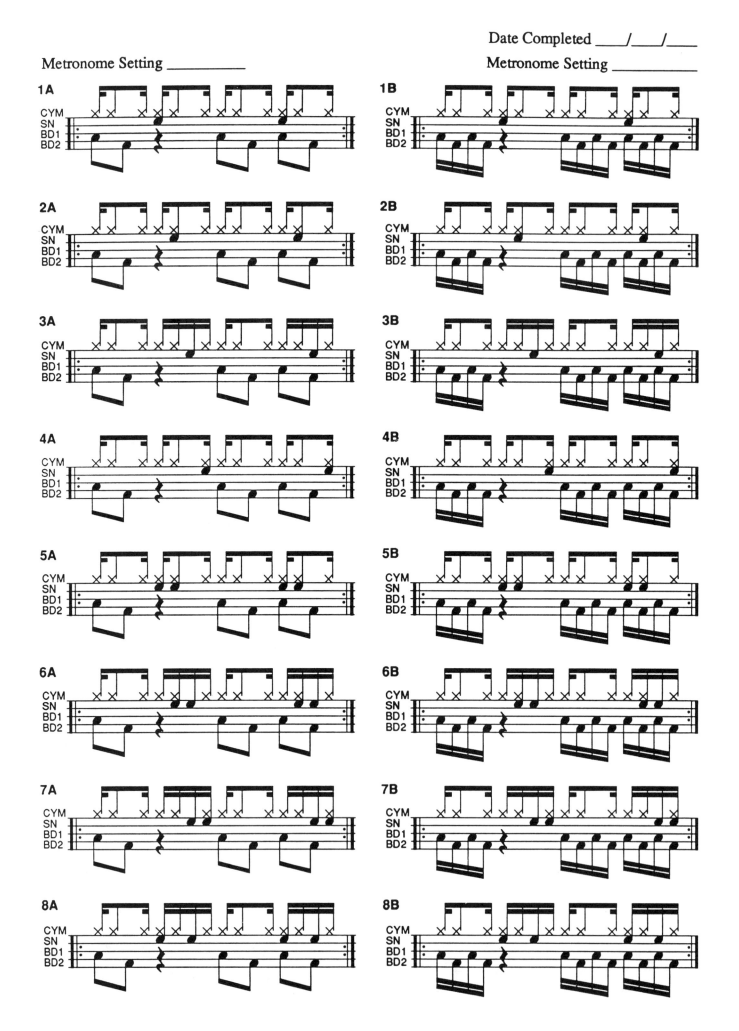

40

Metronome Setting _____

Metronome Setting _____

41

Metronome Setting_____

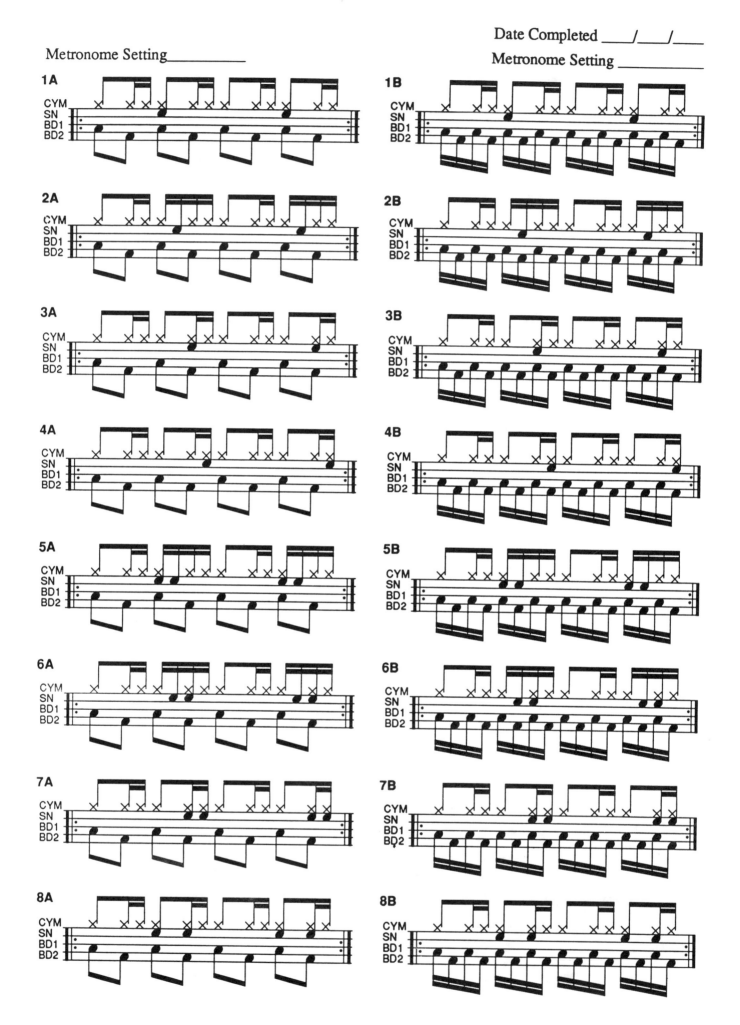

42

Metronome Setting_____

Metronome Setting _____

43

Metronome Setting_____

Metronome Setting _____

Metronome Setting_____

45

Metronome Setting_____

Metronome Setting _____

46

Metronome Setting _____

Metronome Setting _____

Metronome Setting _____

48

Metronome Setting _____

Metronome Setting _____

Metronome Setting _____

Metronome Setting _____

Metronome Setting _____

Metronome Setting _____

Metronome Setting _____

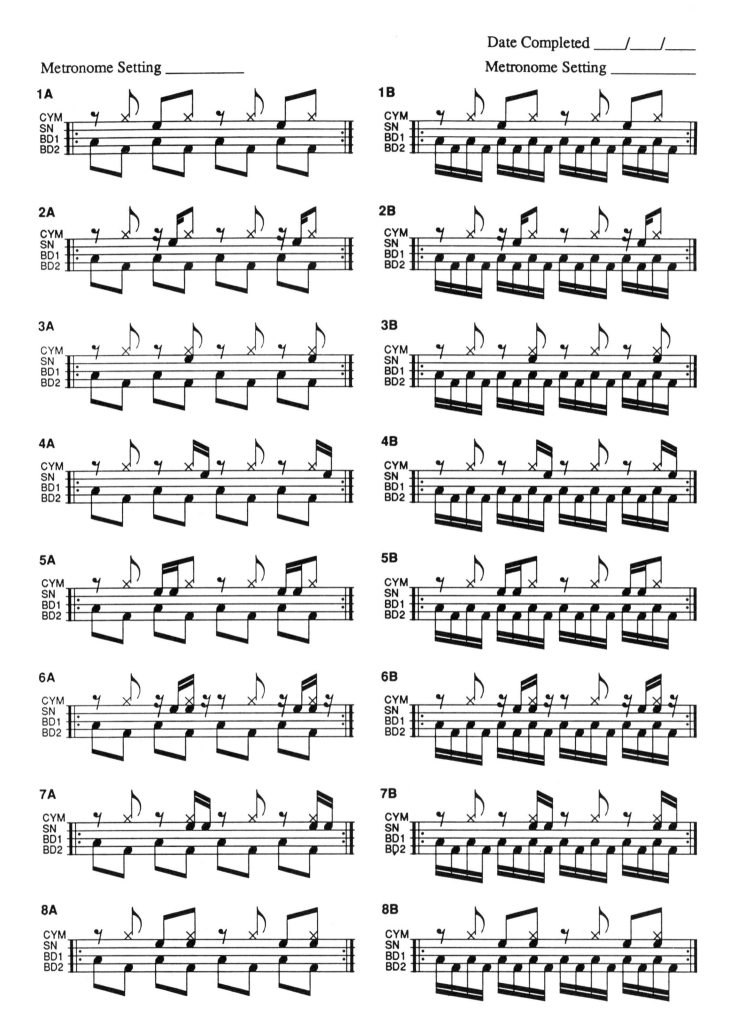

52

Metronome Setting _____

Metronome Setting _____

Metronome Setting _____

54

Metronome Setting _____

Metronome Setting _____

55

Metronome Setting _____

Metronome Setting _____

Metronome Setting _____

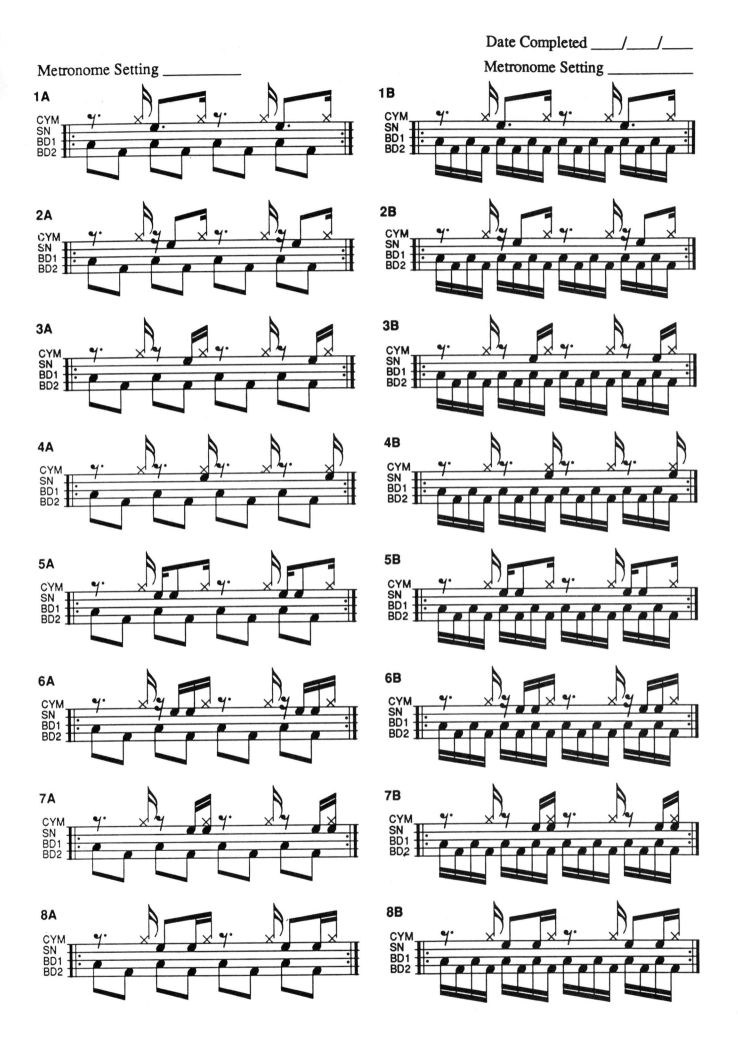

57

Metronome Setting _____

58

Metronome Setting _____

Metronome Setting _____

Metronome Setting _____

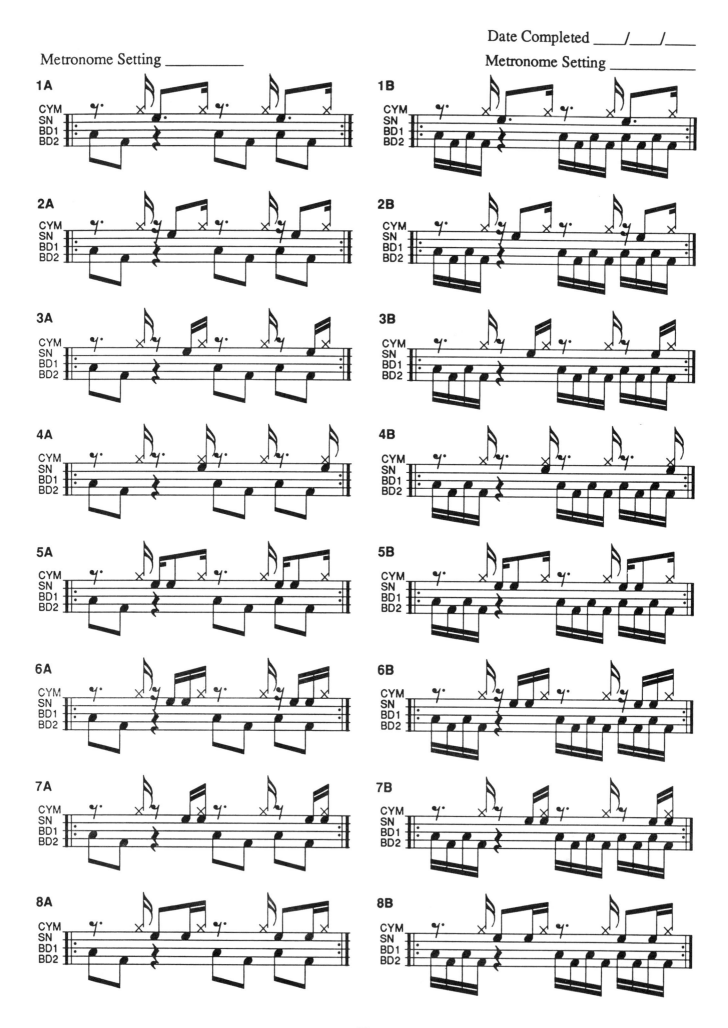

Metronome Setting _____

61

Metronome Setting _____

Metronome Setting _____

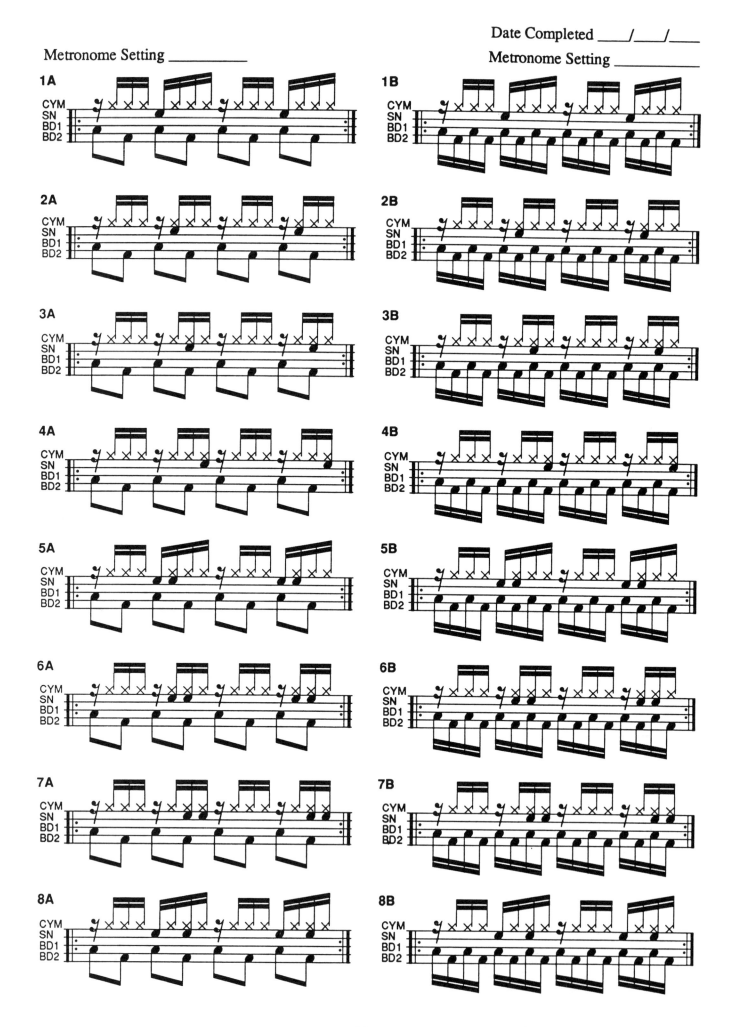

Metronome Setting _____

Metronome Setting _____

Metronome Setting _____   Metronome Setting _____

Metronome Setting _____

Metronome Setting _____

Metronome Setting _____

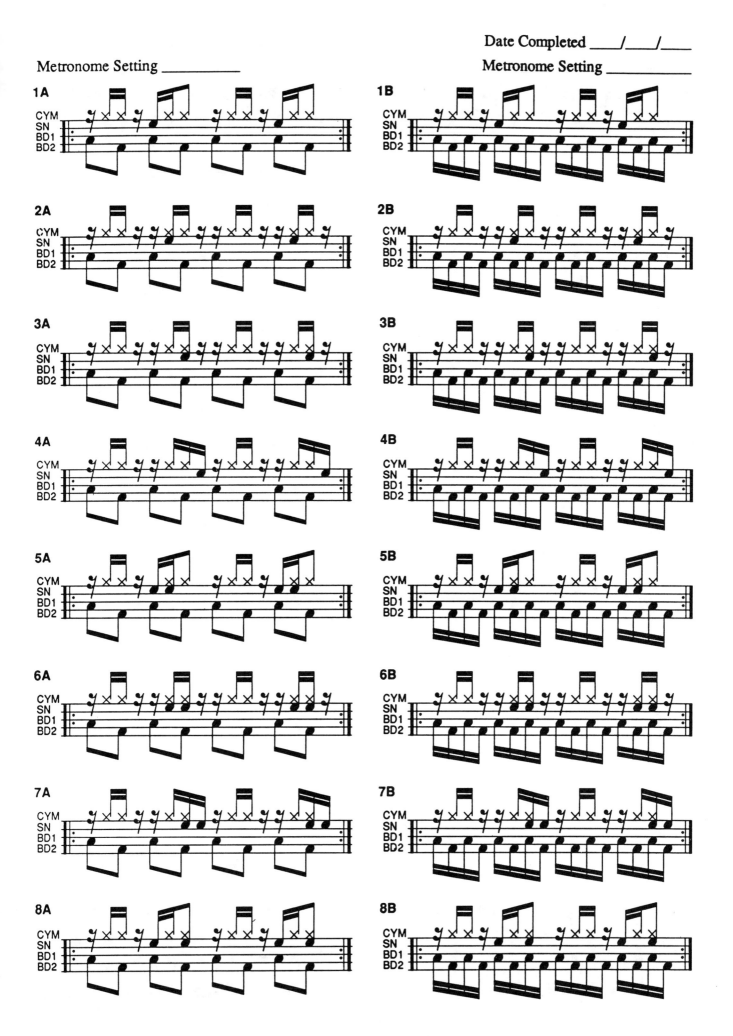

Metronome Setting _____

Metronome Setting _____

Metronome Setting _____

Metronome Setting _____

69

Metronome Setting _____

Metronome Setting _____

Metronome Setting _____

Metronome Setting _____

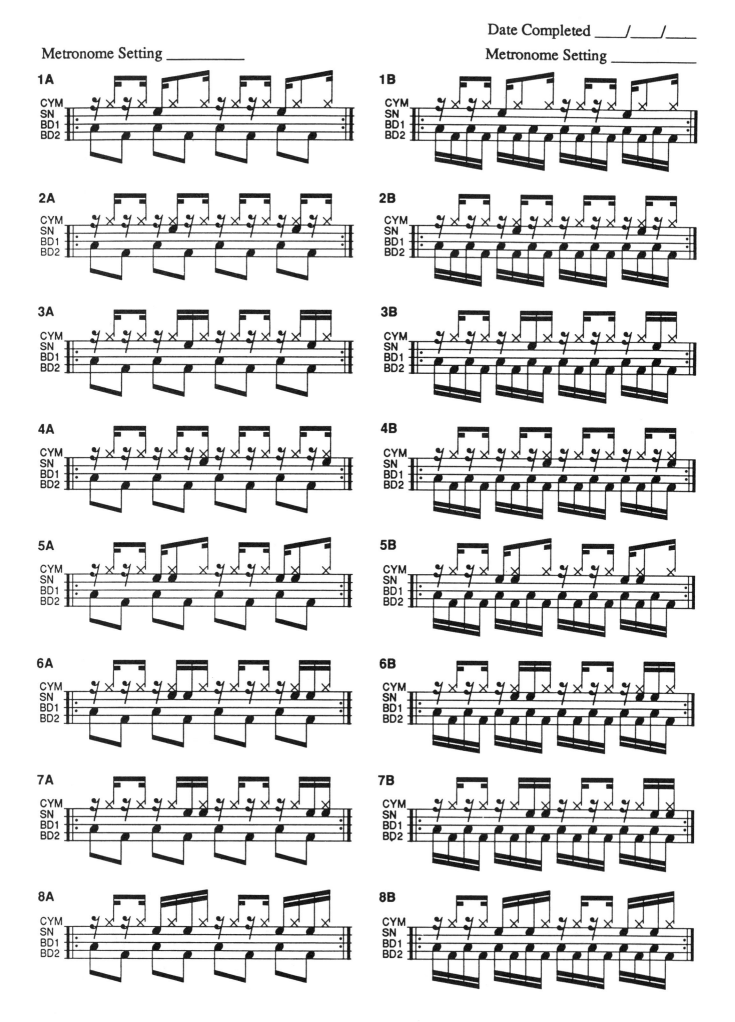

Metronome Setting _____

Metronome Setting _____

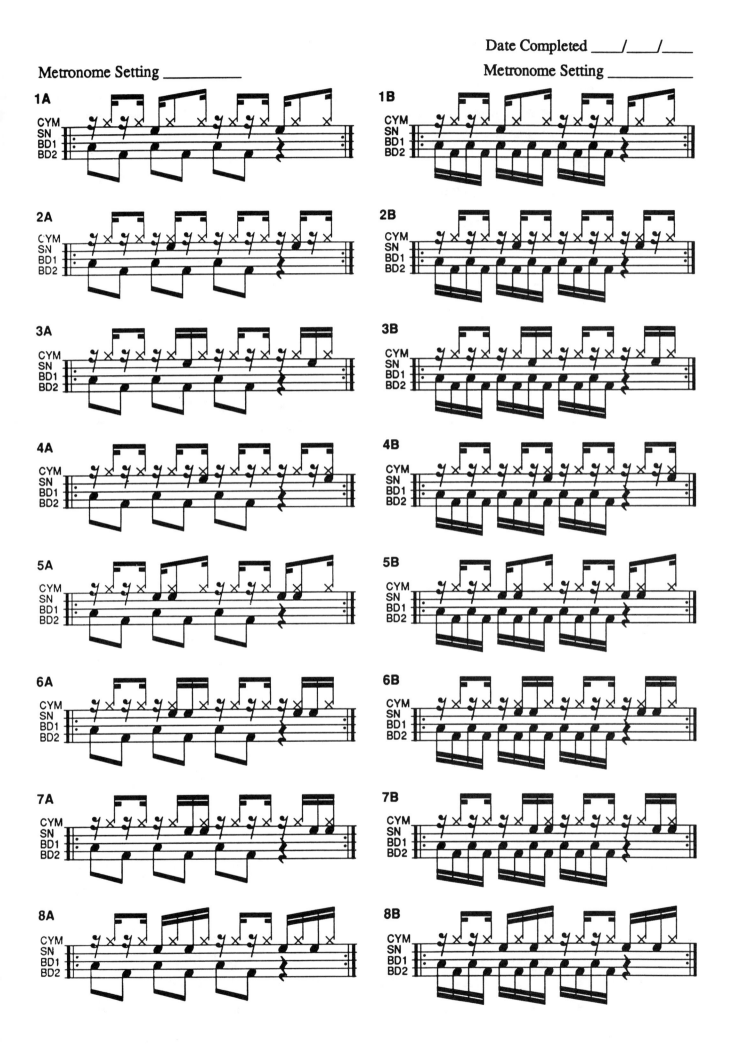

Metronome Setting _____

Metronome Setting _____

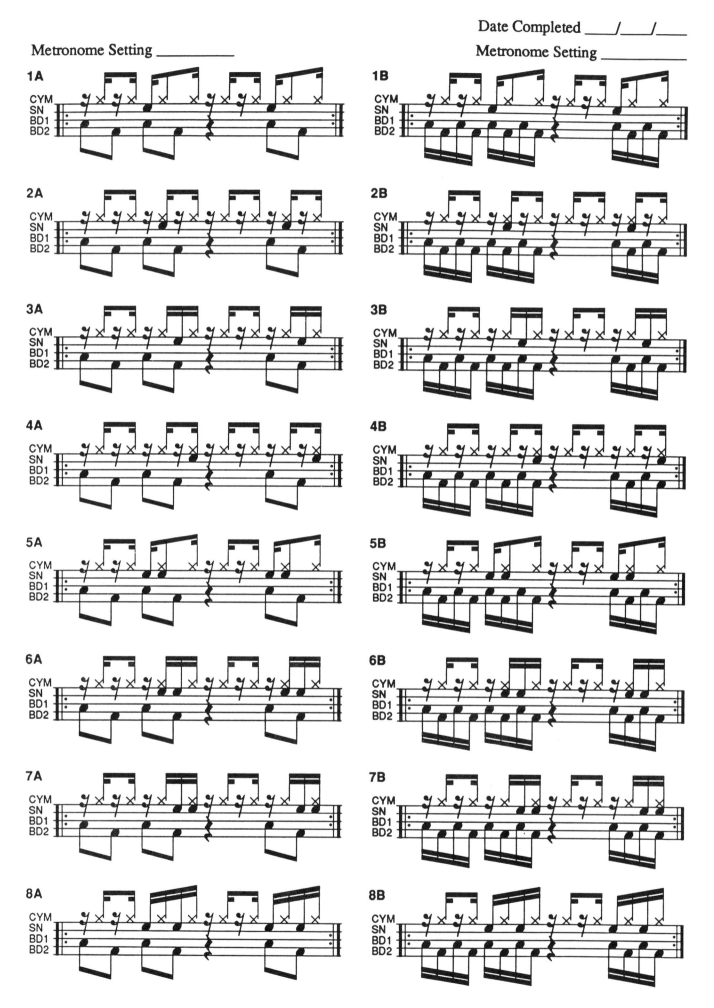

74

Metronome Setting _____

75

Date Completed ____ / ____ / ____

Metronome Setting _____

Metronome Setting _____

76

Metronome Setting _____

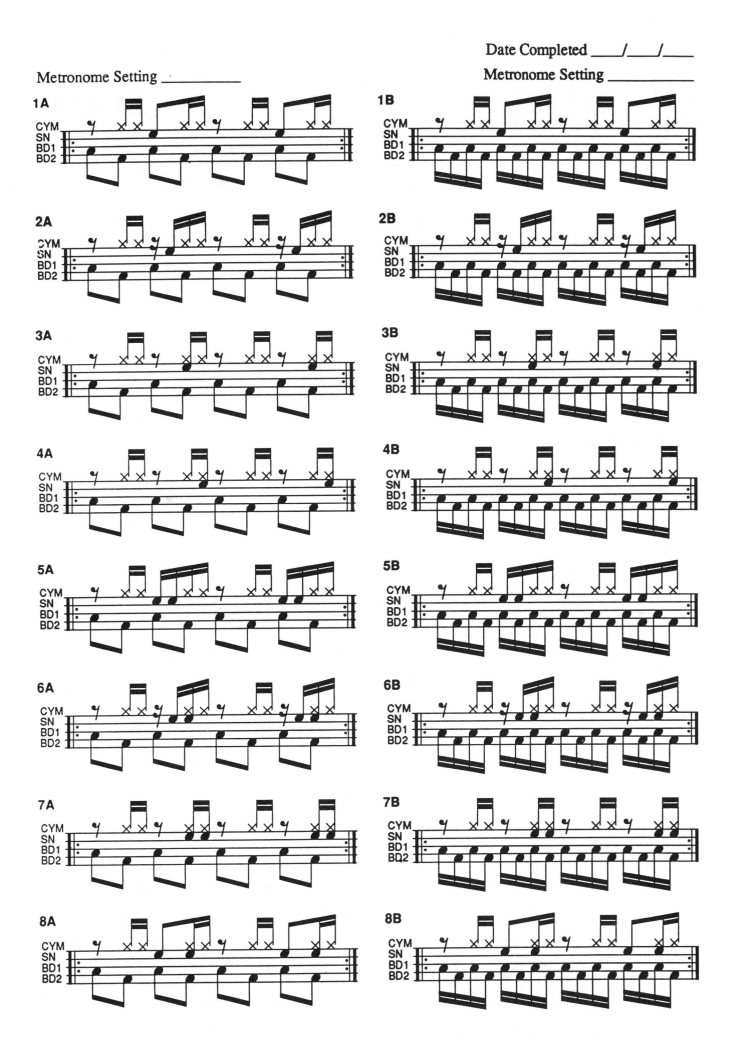

77

Metronome Setting _____

Metronome Setting _____

Metronome Setting _____

# PART II

Complete Double Bass Drum Workout-Part II has been written as an extension of Part I. You are now going to take the "chops" that you developed in the first part, and start applying them in a practical, musical way. Hopefully, as you play the different bass drum patterns in each section, you will pick out certain ones to "file away", and be inspired to try your own ideas. (For instance, the snare drum can be moved all over the place).

The reason that the snare drum stays exclusively on "2" and "4" in Part II, unlike Part I, is that mathematically it would have to be about 600 pages long to accommodate all eight of the snare drum patterns presented in Part I! (That is, if they were combined with the one hundred double bass patterns in this book). That will be up to you to do, but only after you have completed Part II with the snare drum staying on "2" and "4".

The basic layout of Complete Double Bass Drum Workout-Part II is to use the same fifteen hi-hat patterns from Part I combined with one hundred different double bass ideas. Every five pages, the hi-hat pattern will change, and the bass drum patterns from the previous section will repeat in the same order. It's a good idea to use a metronome, especially when you get to the sections where the hi-hat pattern is not right on the beat. In Part I, the eighth notes played on the "A" column of each page put the left foot on the "and" of each beat. This was just to get the left foot started in the easiest way possible. The basic premise of this section, as in column "B" of Part I, is that the dominant foot will always play on the beat and the "and" of each beat, and the secondary foot will always play on the "e" and the "u" of each beat. Also, experiment with using both hands on the hi-hat when playing the straight 16th note pattern and other "busy" patterns. Obviously, the right hand cannot hit the hi-hat and snare drum simultaneously, but the increased speed that you achieve will more than make up for it. Good luck!

83

Date Completed ____/____/____

Metronome Setting _____

84

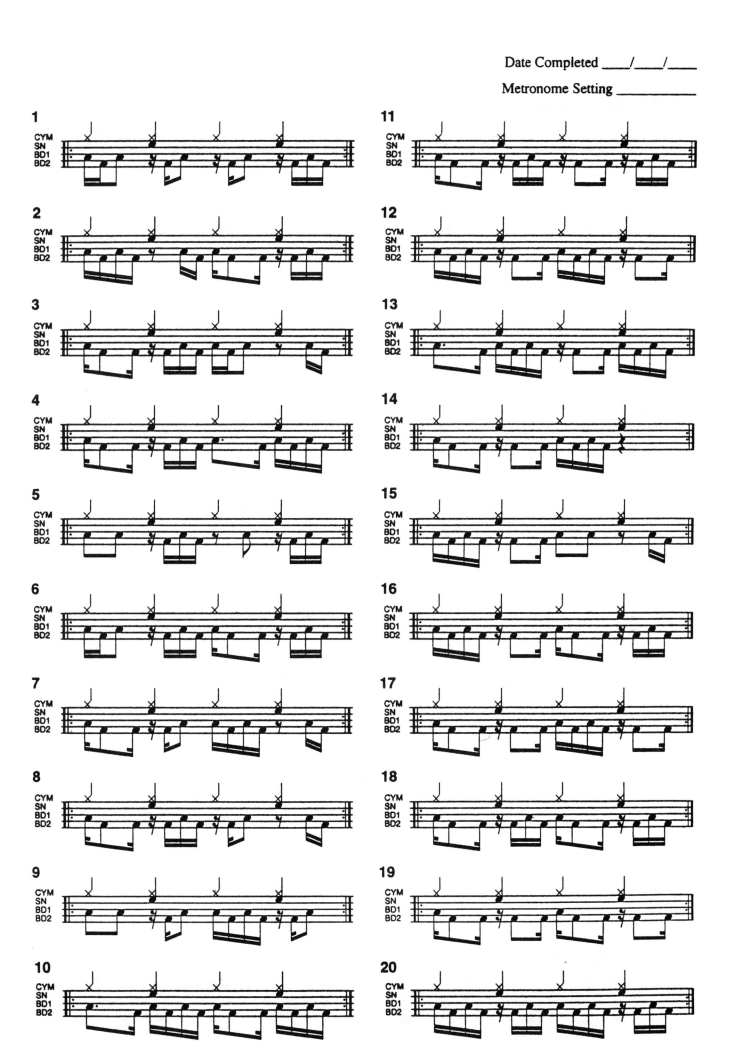

88

89

91

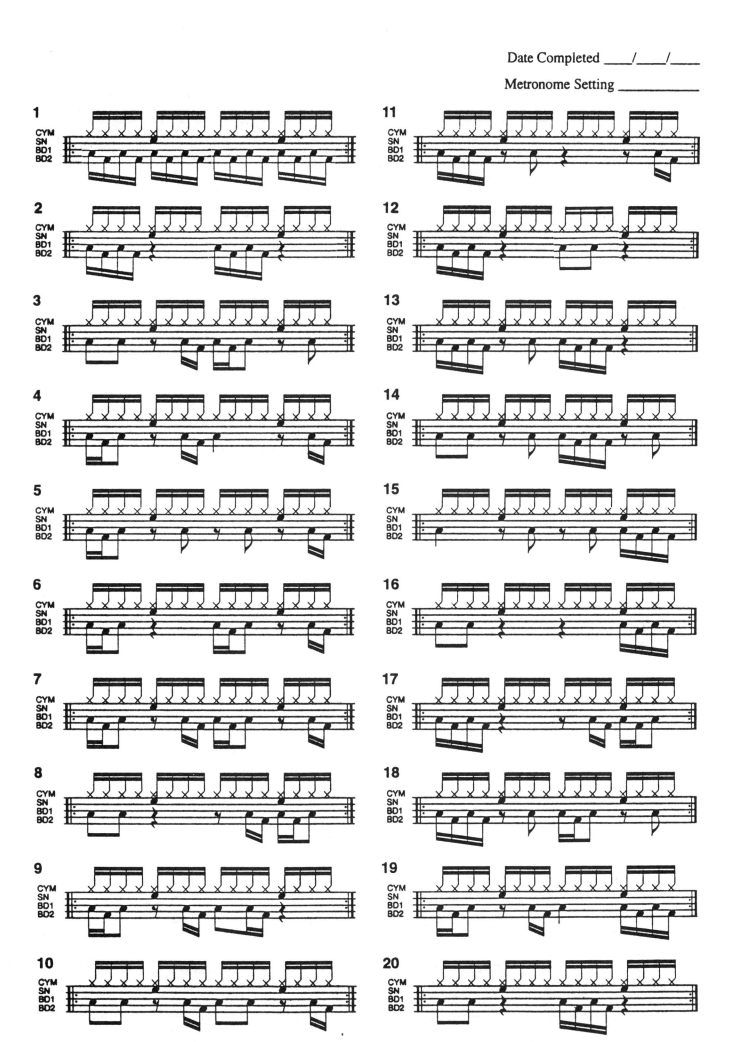

94

95

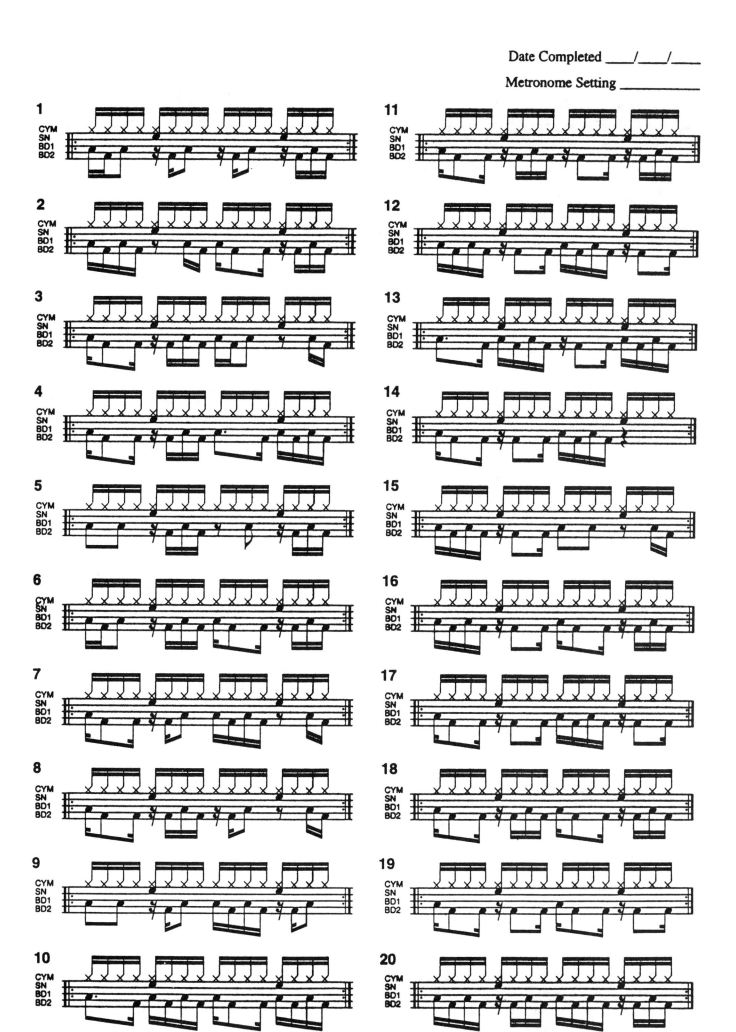

100

101

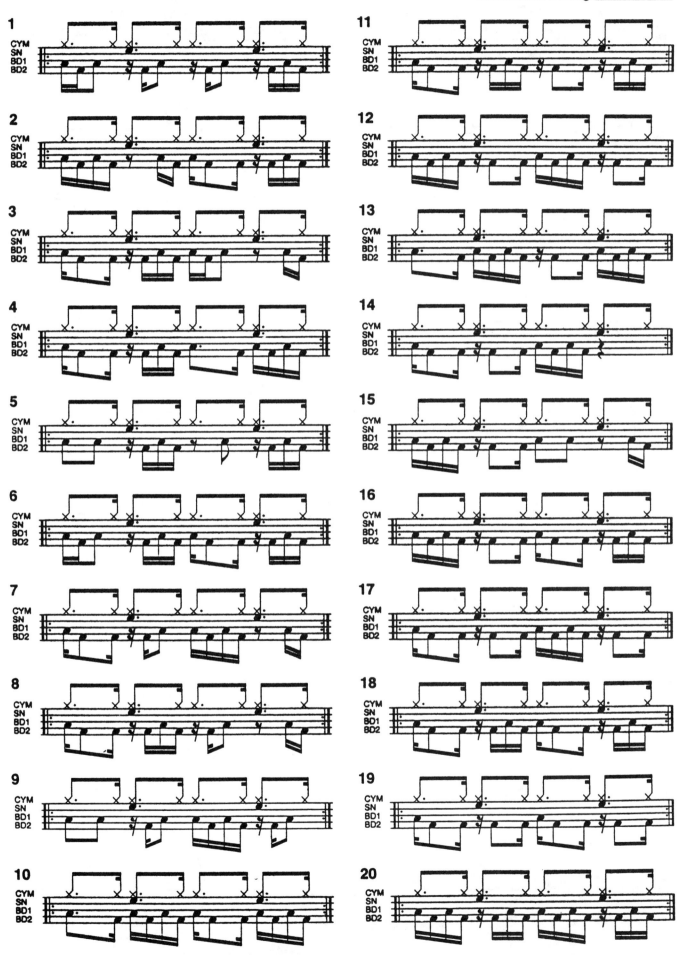

107

108

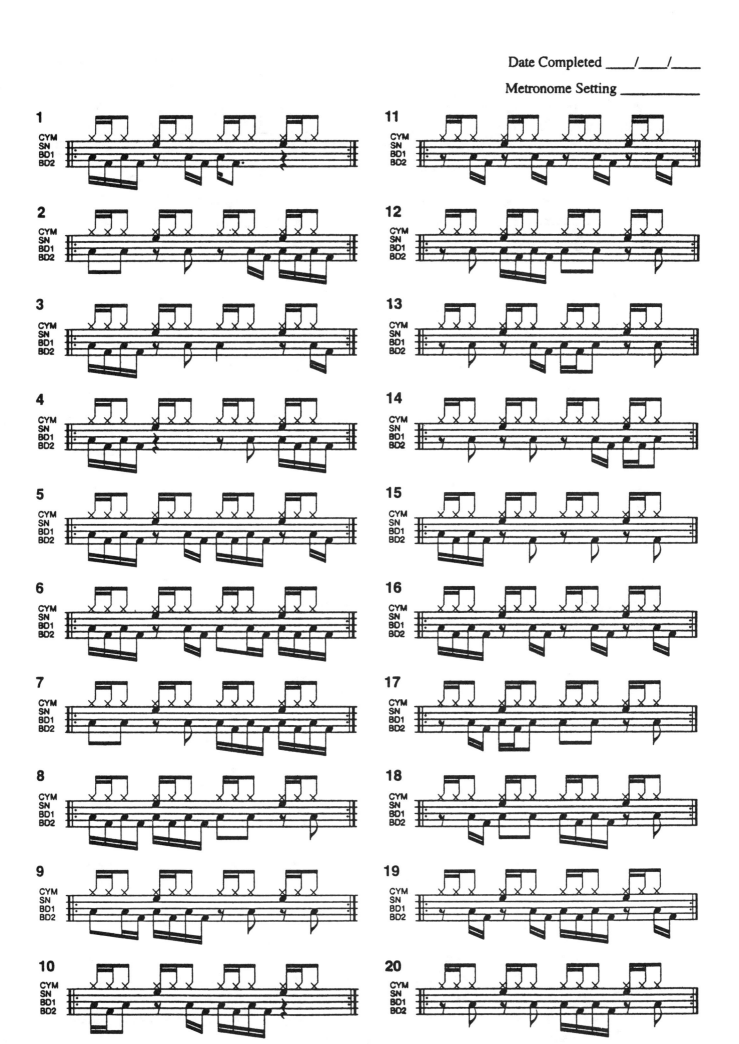

109

110

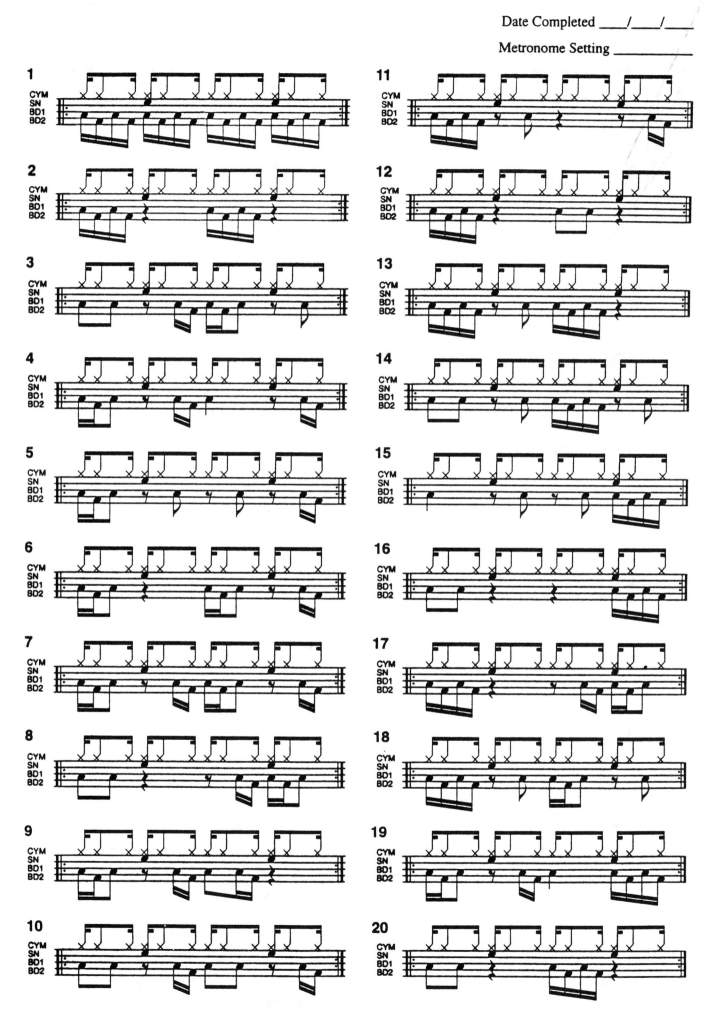

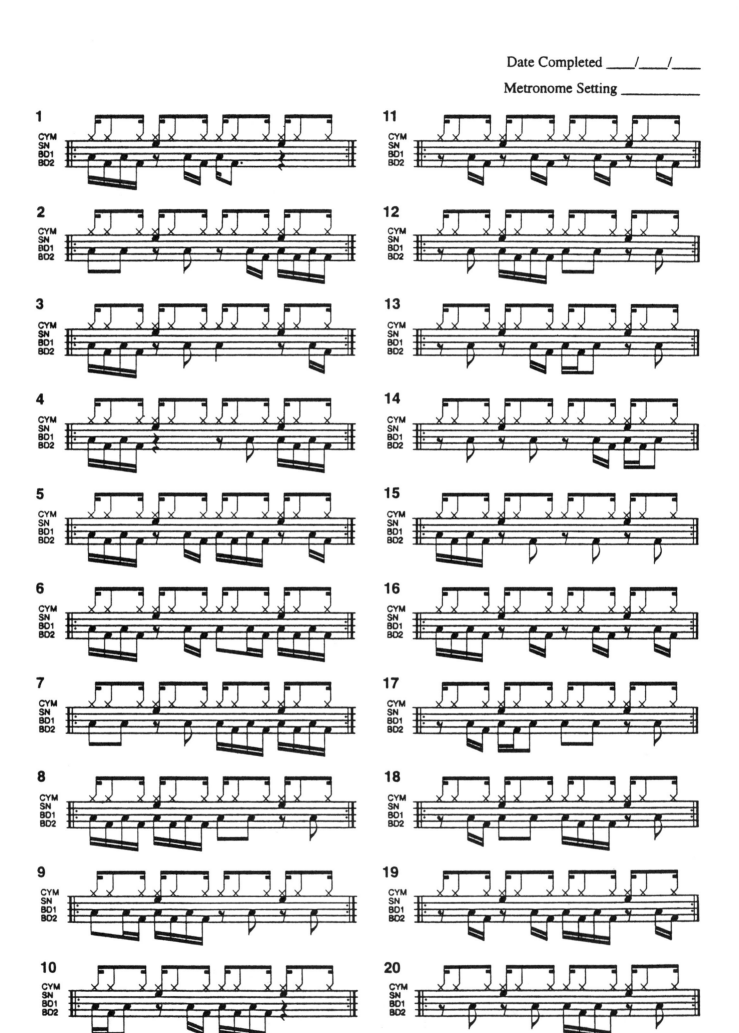

114

115

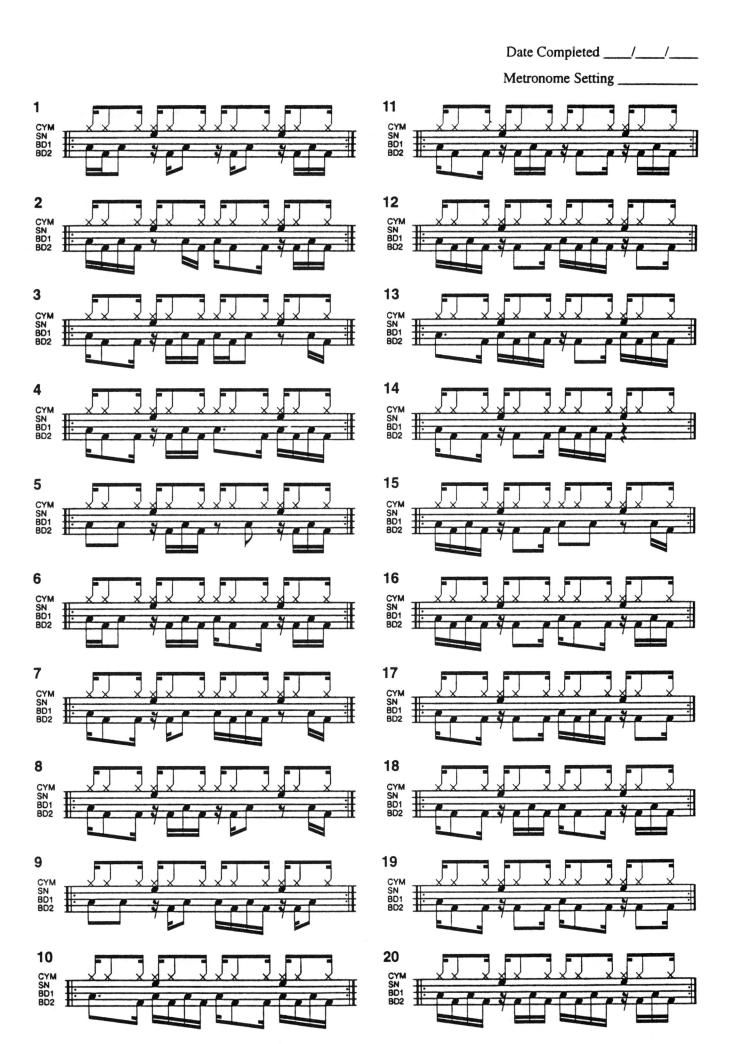

118

119

Date Completed ____/____/____

Metronome Setting _____

120

121

122

123

124

125

126

129

131

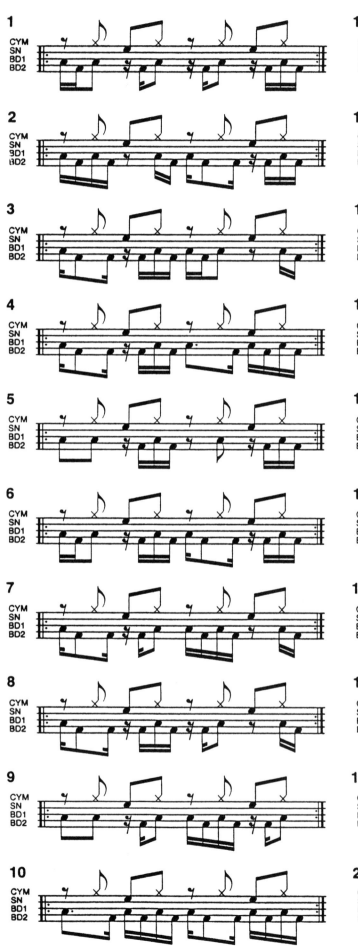

133

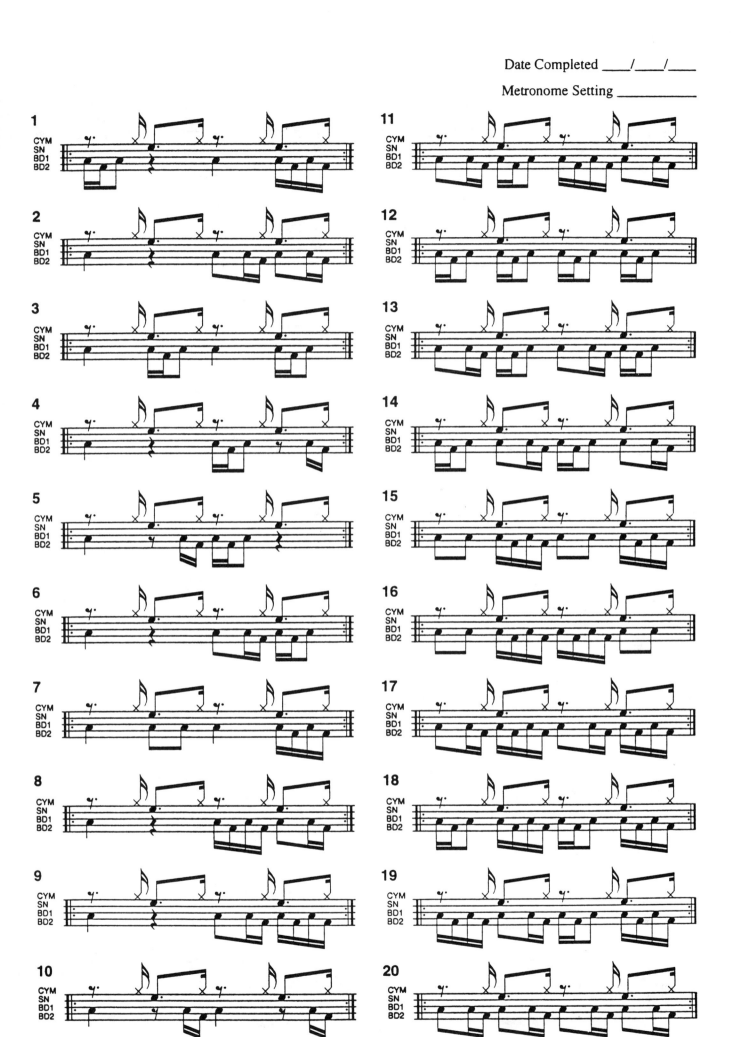

135

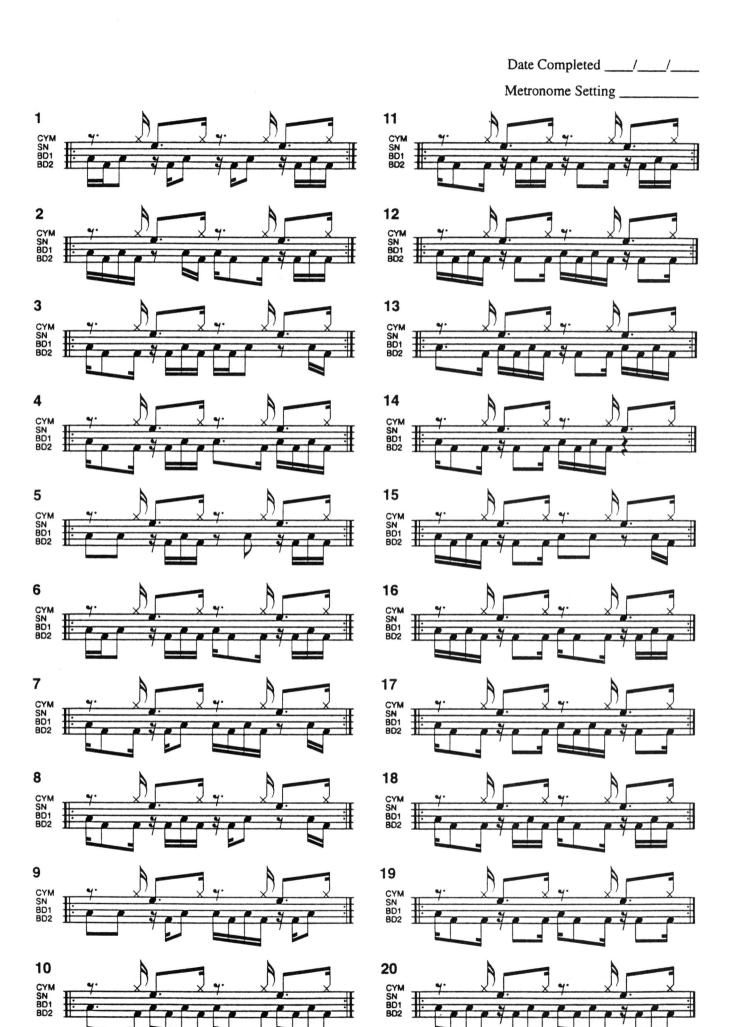

138

139

141

143

147

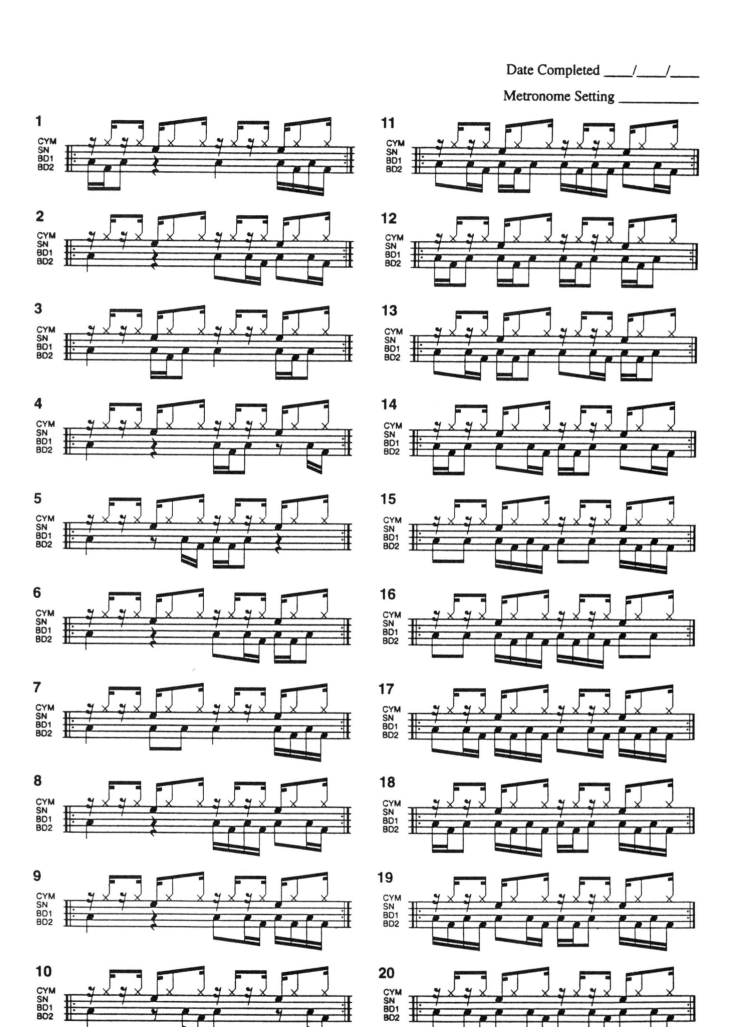

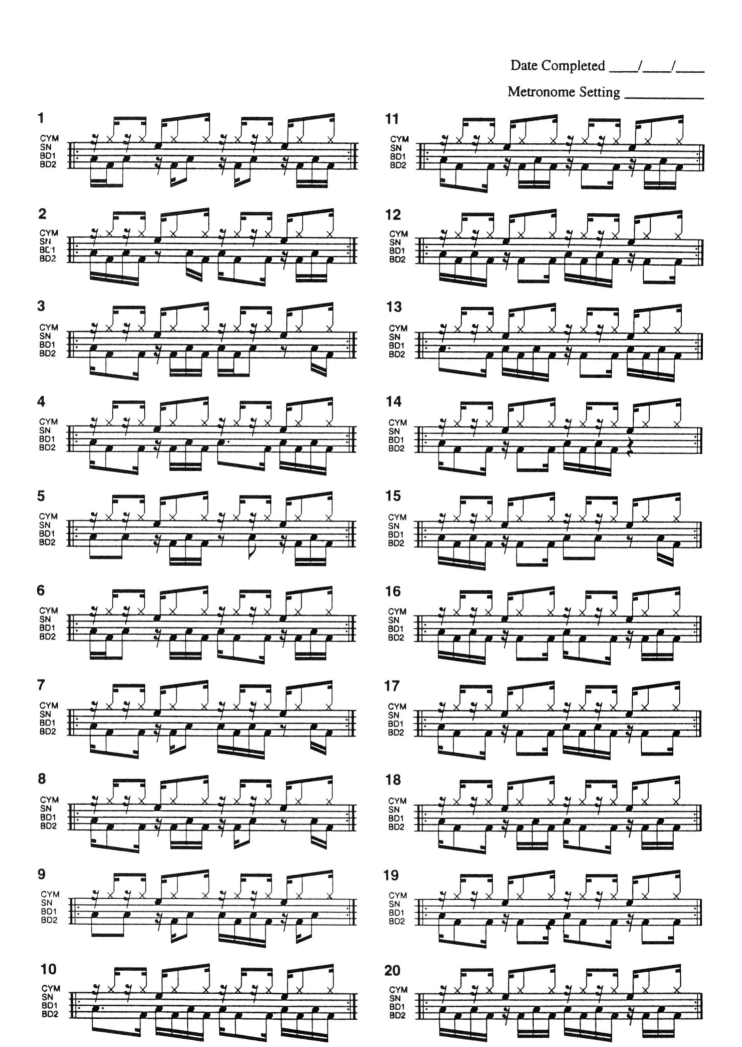

152

153

154